THE AMATEUR ARTIST

SKETCHING THE ENGLISH COUNTRY HOUSE

ROBERT BARGERY

THE GEORGIAN GROUP

THE PICTURES REPRODUCED in this volume are taken from the Pardoe Collection of 17–19th century drawings, watercolours and prints assembled by Bernard Pardoe, The Georgian Group's former treasurer, and given to the Group in 2000 by his widow, Patricia.

The Collection contains images of Georgian buildings and landscapes from across the British Isles, covering everything from palaces and parkland to vernacular buildings and follies.

Many of the descriptions featured in the following pages first appeared in *The Georgian*, the magazine of The Georgian Group, between 2002 and 2016.

First published in 2016
by The Georgian Group in conjunction with Blacker Limited
Text © the author. Images © The Georgian Group 2016

British Library Cataloguing in Publication Data
A catalogue record for this book is available from the British Library

ISBN 978-1-897739-02-0

Contents

Introduction

In amongst copious prints and engravings taken over the years from bound volumes, The Georgian Group's Pardoe Collection of country house images contains about two hundred original works. A small selection is reproduced here, with commentary that seeks to reflect on what is shown rather than recite architectural history.

The drawings were largely done, one supposes, for the private pleasure of the artist – the desultory leisure pursuit of a house guest, perhaps. The works are literally amateur in that way. Are those who produced them artists at all? Yes in a mechanistic sense – they give us representations of reality born of sense impressions. No in the sense that their representations are in the main mere observation or reportage. They do not transport us to another imaginative realm.

But attempted literal representations of country houses are probably more useful to us at this distance. They give us interesting documentary evidence, drawn *en plein air* as a record of fact. Give or take the sometimes serious technical limitations of the artist, we are shown buildings as built. The perspectives are sometimes skewed and there is the odd impossible contortion, but the result is broadly realistic – unpolished but also unmediated. The point is proved by the one exception here to the amateur rule: William Daniell RA. His drawing, of Kings Weston in Somerset, departs from sober fact, offering instead a kind of impressionism, but with greater skill and freedom of expression comes a less useful addition to the historical record.

Another common thread is the helpful tendency to include everything – gardens, immediate surroundings and people, in whom architects are notoriously uninterested except as cut-and-paste automatons. As visual inventories, these pictures are often fuller and more rounded than disciplined architectural drawings, which might differ from the built version and which, as a category of imagery, have no pretensions to a social dimension.

Neither, historically, are architectural drawings the work of women, but we have here contributions by female artists. Amateurism, as we see, is the handmaiden of diversity. Does it also bring amateurishness? Sometimes, yes. There is a *naïveté* to many of the drawings, and not a deliberate one. But that in itself is compelling and adds to the charm. So, too, does the occasional scrapbook quality. Some crude cutting and pasting has gone on over the years, as pictures have been chopped about to fit albums and mounts. Some pictures are double-sided – which the artist intended as *verso* and which as *recto* may not always be clear but later dealers have often made the judgment for them, irreversibly so when the picture has been mutilated or left with inedible adhesive marks. The cover image is one such, but though battered around the edges it sums up the best of the Pardoe Collection, a pleasing snapshot caught unselfconsciously by an accomplished amateur.

Robert Bargery, Secretary of The Georgian Group 2002–2016

Harrington Hall, Lincolnshire

The distinctiveness of Harrington, evident in our watercolour, lies in the bizarre tower that bisects an otherwise fairly textbook proto-Georgian façade dating from 1673. As Pevsner says, 'it projects almost alarmingly'. It is in fact a sixteenth century porch, a remnant of the Elizabethan seat of the Copledykes that was kept by the seventeenth century builder to break up the monotony of the thirteen-bay entrance front. It certainly achieves that, providing a powerful punctuation point in a very horizontal building, but the effect is nonetheless peculiar, partly because the utilitarian plainness of the porch makes it look at first glance like a modern intervention. It is not quite devoid of ornament: as Pevsner also says, 'it is dressed up with an Artisan-Mannerist show face of exceedingly elongated Ionic brick pilasters' which he judges to be a classical flourish dating from the 1660s.

None of this fine detail is discernible in our distant prospect, which depicts the ensemble of hall, church and rectory – more or less the extent, then and now, of what is nominally the hamlet of Harrington, deep in the remote Lincolnshire Wolds; or, alternatively. 'Tennyson Country': it was at Harrington, supposedly, that Tennyson developed an infatuation with Rosa Baring, giving rise to the immortal quatrain "Come into the garden, Maud / For the black bat, Night, has flown / Come into the garden, Maud / I am here at the gate alone"

The rustic idyll is still perfectly intact, at least to outward appearances. The hall suffered a catastrophic fire in 1991 but was meticulously restored and retains its Grade I listing – proof that piecing back a charred interior is a practical proposition. Nowadays the hall is again a private home and Lincoln Red cattle graze in place of sheep. Aside from that, the only point of difference is the church, which S. S. Teulon rebuilt in 1854. In the process he raised the tower; our picture shows its mediaeval predecessor, complete with corner finials that Teulon replaced with buttresses for his new upper stage.

Watercolour, unknown artist; 9 × 6 ins

Hales Place, Kent

Our artist has taken the vantage point that best shows Hales' palatial extent – across the parkland, seen flanked by its massive coach and stable blocks with their Diocletian windows, a recurrent motif of neo-Palladian stabling ever since Kent popularised it at Houghton. A suitably awed observer in 1773 said that the brand new house was 'more fit for the residence of a monarch than for a simple country gentleman'. In the nineteenth century the volume increased even further, though at some expense of elegance, with the addition of substantial infill blocks between the main house and pavilions.

The 'simple country gentleman' was Sir Edward Hales, who inherited an Elizabethan property on an adjacent site and built this powerhouse to replace it. He might have been motivated by a wish to rebuild the family's position, both physically and metaphorically. That position had fallen away over the previous hundred years, albeit from an elevated point. An attempted disinheritance and firesales of houses had left things a relative mess.

From contemporary accounts, Hales Place had the desired effect of re-establishing lost status, partly because what seems here to be a resolutely *country* house in vast parkland was in fact only a mile from Canterbury and was thus a visible advertisement of wealth. Another early visitor, also impressed, said that Hales was 'of a fine height, and extends 538 feet in length, having a terrace and spacious lawn in front. It commands a most beautiful view of the city of Canterbury, its cathedral, and the neighbouring country'. The view, of course, worked both ways.

Things took an idiosyncratic turn with Sir Edward's great-niece Mary, who inherited in 1837 at the age of one and in due time used Hales as a testbed for various slightly scatty religious projects. An abortive attempt to make the house a Carmelite nunnery was followed by a longer flirtation with the Benedictines. After her death, Hales was bought at auction by Jesuits from Lyons, who extended it to form St Mary's College but left in 1924. Hales's proximity to Canterbury then proved its undoing: speculative developers bought the land for housing and demolition (in 1930) inevitably followed. The suburb that now occupies the site is a labyrinth of *culs-de-sac* but still bears the name Hales Place. We are left with this as one of a very few images to show Hales in its short-lived pomp as a magnificent private house.

Watercolour, unknown artist; 10 × 6 ins

Kirkstall Grange, West Riding

Kirkstall was designed by James Paine for Walter Wade in the early 1750s. Sir Howard Colvin, notably fastidious, merely attributes Kirkstall to Paine rather than according him definite authorship, so the evidence is not watertight, but stylistically it fits. Everything characteristic of Paine is here, from the conceptual sweep of the compact villa form and the elevation of the Kentian pavilion (as at Holkham) into a principal block, down to the details: the dominant, full-width pediment, the broken cornice and the niche on the entrance front.

The sketch is annotated *verso*, in a contemporary hand, 'Kirkstall Grange, Residence of Willliam Beckett Esq., M.P.' The Becketts, High-Victorian bankers, lived there from the 1830s, renaming it Beckett's Park, and made numerous, typically assertive interventions in the 1830s and the 1850s, notably the *porte-cochère* and a succession of canted bay windows. Our drawing shows some but not all of them (ground-floor bays were also added to the five-bay side elevation) and probably dates from the early 1850s.

These Victorian excrescences have compromised the masculine classical purity of Paine's design, although enough surface personality survives to allow it still to read as a Paine production. And in truth their effect is not readily apparent in our drawing, which downplays the three added bays on the entrance front to the point of invisibility. There are other infelicities: the artist makes the left-hand addition resemble a tacked-on cottage *orné* whereas in reality it is an elegant and beautifully-conceived classical pavilion. The modillion cornice is

vastly exaggerated – it looks as deep-eaved and barn-like as Inigo Jones's at St Paul's Covent Garden but is actually fairly modest and proportionate. And the lead-covered roof dome, also a fairly discreet affair, appears here a bulbous feature, almost as if an observatory. In the foreground, lightly pencilled and disconnected from the main drawing as if an independent afterthought, is a low garden wall surmounted by urns and sphinxes.

The house and its surroundings have survived reasonably well given the proximity to Leeds. It now sits within the relatively sylvan setting of the campus of Leeds Metropolitan University and the early twentieth century redbrick hall of residence that occupies its back garden is sufficiently competent a piece of varsity architecture to allow Paine's villa to be enjoyed without undue distraction.

Watercolour, unknown artist; 9 × 6 ins

Denham Place, Buckinghamshire

Denham Place, two miles north of Uxbridge, was built 1688–1701 for Sir Roger Hill, probably by William Stanton, and passed in the mid-eighteenth century to the Way family. By the time of this watercolour, in 1826, it was owned by Benjamin Way, who was shortly (in the 1830s) to undertake alterations that disposed of the rooftop balustrade. The landscape park, possibly by Capability Brown and replacing a formal late seventeenth century garden, was another initiative of his, and as part of that work the entrance front (shown here) was reoriented from west to east.

1826 was the year that Way's only child, Catherine, married Sir Montague Cholmeley Bt. He died only five years later, aged fifty-eight, and Catherine died childless in 1864. On the reverse of this picture is a pencil inscription: 'Given by Aunt Cholmeley Jan 1864.' Might the woman in the picture (clearly a fashionable dresser, with her up-to-the-minute elaborate bonnet and corseted waist) be Catherine, depicted in the year she left Denham on her marriage, symbolically pointing to a future away from the house? Evidently she kept the drawing, returning it to Denham (where branches of the Way family remained until 1920) only late in life.

If that speculation is right, the painting had a purpose for the artist beyond one of pure architectural record, which might explain the amateurishness in the depiction of the building. Though charming and painstaking, the composition is neither especially accomplished (the perpendiculars are wilfully awry) nor very accurate.

The door, with its carved stone entablature, is peculiarly undersized. In reality, the bust in the centre of the broken pediment reaches the string course, though here it is shown no higher than the sashes either side. The quoins are in fact rubbed brick but seem here to be stone; the window heads are also red brick but again are drawn a lighter colour. The wood-moulded modillion cornice is deeper than it appears here and the egg and dart bed-mould less pronounced.

One interesting detail, presumably depicted accurately, is the design of the dormers. Here they are alternately segmental-headed and pedimented. A *Country Life* photograph of 1925 shows them all flat-headed. When the dormers were restored in the twentieth century, those in the five-bay central section were given alternate segmental and pedimented heads but those in the wings were all pedimented. An error or a deliberate deviation from the original?

Later in the nineteenth century, the entrance steps acquired balustrading on either side and a tall slender brick chimney (still there in 1925, but now gone) was added almost over the eaves between the left-hand pair of dormers in the five-bay central range.

Watercolour, unknown artist, 1826; 7 × 5 ins

Storrs Hall, Westmorland

This watercolour of Storrs, a classical villa on the banks of Lake Windermere, is by John Chessell Buckler (1793–1894), also an accomplished architect whose buildings include Costessey Hall in Norfolk (1826) and Butleigh Court in Somerset (1845). Originally built for Sir John Legard in the mid 1790s, Storrs was largely redesigned by Joseph Gandy for John Bolton in 1808–9. Given that William Wilberforce, the leading slave trade abolitionist, had been to Storrs to visit Legard, it is ironic that the house should have been bought by Bolton, the leading West India merchant of his generation and a major player in the slave trade. His annual profits, rarely below £38,000, financed the expansion of Storrs.

The view here shows Gandy's north (entrance) front, still intact today and a good example of his idiosyncratic treatment of classical forms. The central three-bay portion is the original 1790s house. Gandy added the wings to east and west, slightly taller than the original house and projecting to north and south. His signature is evident in the tripartite ground-floor windows with thick scrolled console brackets supporting triangular pediments; the first-floor windows with their moulded surrounds terminating in block capitals; and especially the exotic loggia, a Greek Doric composition with fluted Samian columns. The entablature supports a parapet of fleshy lotus buds and the doorway, just visible here, is crowned by four console brackets below an entablature decorated with stylised rosettes. Visible above the roofline is Gandy's dramatic central rotunda, the *pièce de resistance* of the interior. The house is now an hotel.

North View of Storrs Hall, Windermere, Westmoreland.
The Seat of John Bolton Esqr.

Pencil and watercolour, by J C Buckler; 12 × 9 ins

Gumley Hall, Leicestershire

No architect is known for Gumley, built in 1764 for Joseph Cradock near Market Harborough, but it is clear that the house was a lifelong project: as late as 1791, Throsby's *Leicestershire* notes that the 'the whole of the rooms are not fitted up' and the house was still unfinished, at least internally, at Cradock's death in 1826. Throsby also notes the quality of the library and the paintings ('in a good parlour, I saw a fine picture, said to be done by Guido'); probably Cradock saw himself more as a bibliophile-cum-thespian than as an architect and decorator, but the main reason for the lack of progress was the worsening state of his finances.

His *DNB* entry says that he built Gumley 'upon a scale which led to embarrassment' and records that 'in 1823 growing embarrassments induced him to sell his estate and library and retire to London on a small annuity'. The entry describes a lively and dilettantish existence: the windows at his London house in Dean Street, Soho, were broken by a mob in the 1770s after he wrote disobligingly about John Wilkes; he gave private theatricals at Gumley, 'where Garrick, to whom he is described as being a sort of twin brother, offered to play the Ghost to his Hamlet', and his musical skill 'procured him a welcome at Lord Sandwich's seat at Hinchinbroke, where Miss Ray sang in oratorios, while Lord Sandwich performed on the kettledrum'. And he 'amused himself with landscape gardening', an interest hinted at by the three industrious gardeners in the picture. The *Victoria County History* (1964) records that he 'laid out the gardens and

plantations of Gumley Hall in imitation of the Parc de St. Cloud and in the summer months they became a fashionable resort for the gentry of Leicester, particularly those who came to take the mineral waters of its 'spa', a chalybeate spring found in 1789'.

Gumley (built of Leicestershire red brick, although it appears more as stone in the picture) was remodelled in 1870, when a full-width Tuscan colonnade was added to the front shown here and the front door was moved, oddly, to the second bay on the left. At the same time, the northern flanking pavilion (not shown here) was extended to accommodate larger stables and a flamboyant Italianate campanile. The rectory, which stood hard against the Hall, was demolished for the purpose and was rebuilt in a field north of the church. The story of the Hall's decline is wearily familiar: after increasingly rapid changes of ownership it was used for Special Operations Executive training during the War, then as the first Cheshire Home before eventual demolition in 1964. The surroundings, though, are more or less intact: between the church and the campanile, which survives, is simply a grassy gap where the Hall once stood.

Watercolour, unknown artist; 12 × 7 ins

Dagenhams, Essex

Dagnam Park (*sic*) now sits on the eastern extremity of the London conurbation, a municipal buffer between Romford and the M25, fully absorbed into a tamed landscape of golf courses and dormitory suburbs. Save for a couple of forlorn gate piers, the roughly circular lily pond and unseen foundations, no reminders are left of Dagenhams, the house that stood here; occupied by the army during the war, it was demolished in 1950 and a tangled copse now covers the mangled corpse. Thus, abruptly and ignominiously, has ended a long history.

The Dagenham manor was named after the De Dakenham family and later became a Northumberland seat: the 1443 rolls record an order from Henry VI to Henry Percy, 2nd earl and a committed Lancastrian, to go no farther from London than his manor at Dagenham, on pain of a fine. A moated and gabled house, set around a courtyard, was recorded in 1633; in about 1660 Sir Henry Wright had it rebuilt, on a comparatively modest scale but impressively enough for Pepys, who visited in 1665, to praise it as the most notable and pretty house, for its size, that he had seen.

Edward Carteret extended it in the 1730s for Henry Muilman, adding a private chapel, and by 1771 the house consisted of twenty-one bays arranged over two storeys, the central block having an attic storey and a pediment incorporating a lunette. It is this house, an aggrandisement of the seventeenth century building, that we see illustrated; and the watercolour, showing the south front looking east to St Peter's South Weald, is an interesting record, because the building as depicted had a short life, being demolished in the 1770s by a new owner, Sir Richard Neave, later Governor of the Bank of England, who replaced it with a three-storey, nine bay house that faced north, away from the pond. Such frenetic renewal was typical of the Havering area in the eighteenth century, as wealthy bankers and merchants moved out of London, buying old established manors around the Royal demesne of Havering Palace and replacing them with fashionable country seats. Alongside Dagenhams were Flitcroft's Bower House at Havering-atte-Bower, Hare Hall by Paine (1769) and Bedfords for John Heaton (1771), among several others.

Pencil and watercolour, unknown artist; 9 × 6 ins

Benham Park, Berkshire

Our picture shows a charmingly haphazard portrayal of one of the pairs of entrance gates at Benham Park, near Newbury. Inscribed 'The Lodge entrance to the park at Benham, the Seat of His Serene Highness The Margrave Anspach and Bareith [sic Bayreuth]', this amateur watercolour is unsigned and undated but is presumably contemporary with the Margrave's occupation, which lasted from 1798, when he bought Benham from the Cravens, to 1806, when he died there.

The Margrave arrived in England as a private citizen in 1791, having abdicated his margravate and allowed it to be annexed into the Kingdom of Prussia in return for an annual stipend of 300,000 guilders. In the same year he married – a mere fortnight after the death of her husband, from whom she had long been separated – the colourful Lady Craven, whose first husband, the 6th Lord Craven, had commissioned Benham from Henry Holland and Capability Brown in 1771. She retook possession of her old marital home when, via the Margrave, she acquired it from her son, the 7th Lord Craven, in 1798 and she continued living there, as Margravine of Anspach, after the Margrave's death. Horace Walpole called her '*infinitamente* indiscreet', not necessarily a fault in his eyes: by way of solidarity he published, at his Strawberry Hill press, her comedy *Somnambule*, though not her next book, *Modern Anecdotes of the Family of Kinvervankotsprakengatchdern*, a caricature of German pomposity.

The two fine piers shown here have Doric half-columns, decorated with banded rustication, beneath pediments with crossed palms in the tympana; the architraves bear the legend *Salus popula* [sic *populi*] *salus mea*, or 'the welfare of the people is my salvation', an appropriately patrician inscription for a noble governor. This inscription (not, incidentally, the Craven family motto) does not survive and the lodges were extended and remodelled in the late nineteenth century, making them a slightly less harmonious (though still attractive) complement to the piers than the plain stone lodges shown in our picture. The wooden gates have also been replaced with larger and more robust wrought iron models. The piers themselves still form an imposing entrance to the estate, though perhaps even they are upstaged by Benham's other gates; these have late seventeenth century piers brought from Hamstead Marshall (the adjoining Craven estate, just the other side of the River Kennet) and are surmounted by fantastical trophies incorporating armour, weaponry and standards.

Benham Park itself survives but is not currently a private residence, having been converted to offices in 1983.

Watercolour, unknown artist; 9 × 5 ins

Calcot Park, Berkshire

This watercolour of Calcot Park, built for Sir John Blagrave in 1755, is interesting not least for the evidence it provides of its appearance before radical remodelling in the nineteenth century, when the hipped roof shown here was replaced by a curious, not to say absurd, attic storey topped by a shallow hipped roof, leaving a design that was distinctly compromised, especially in profile. At the same time, the lunette in the deeply-dentilled pediment was replaced with an unconvincing sub-Venetian window that appears cramped. The roof, indeed, plays a prominent and bizarre part in the history of the house: when the previous owner, Benjamin Child, sold it to Blagrave, he apparently changed his mind at the last moment and was prevailed upon to leave only by the removal of the lead from the roof. Apocryphally, the damage forced Blagrave to demolish and rebuild, resulting in the present house. Child kept the easternmost part of the estate, now Prospect Park, where he aggrandized a farmhouse as his new seat; that too was short-lived, being replaced by the present bright-white Regency villa, a kind of poor man's Goodwood known as the Mansion House.

Visible to either side in our picture are two of four substantial corner pavilions that form a three-sided stable court extending direct from the rear elevation. Again, the Victorian alterations have slightly spoiled their relationship to the house by altering the relative proportions; they now appear squatter than intended.

Contrary to the impression of ashlar given here, Calcot is red brick, with finely-gauged pilasters below stone Ionic capitals, cornice and pediment – all now also painted bright white, to the aesthetic detriment of the house. The park, stocked here with an impressive array of fallow deer, is now a featureless lawn, in keeping with the successive use of the house since 1930 as a golf clubhouse and, latterly, as apartments. But the deer reflect a once-extensive estate, now much reduced; the rump is surrounded, a little depressingly, by the banal *culs-de-sac* of Reading's western suburbs, but the house at least still sits within an approximation of a parkland setting.

Watercolour, unknown artist; 10 × 7 ins

Berry Head House, Devon

Berry Head House, just east of Brixham on the south Devon coast, was built in 1809 as a military hospital to serve the Napoleonic forts that colonised Berry Head from 1794 onwards. The fact that those Georgian fortifications destroyed an Iron Age hill fort is testament to the longstanding strategic importance of the site, which faces east across the Channel and commands the natural harbour of Tor Bay. Bulwarks had been built here under Henry VIII and Prince William of Orange landed nearby in 1688 to launch the Glorious Revolution from Brixham, so naturally this stretch of coast was deemed a point of vulnerability when the threat of French invasion arose a century later, becoming especially acute in the first decade of the nineteenth century. With the Royal Navy anchored below in Tor Bay, Berry Head was once again a prime defensive position.

The hospital, built on a shallow E plan with a colonnade between the projecting end bays, was protectively sited slightly west of Berry Head itself, on Shoalstone Point in the lee of the Georgian redoubts. Very probably it is the work of Lt. Col. Alexander Mercer, Commanding Engineer at Devonport, who had earlier designed the battery buildings and who was instructed in 1808 to find a site for a hospital. He reported that 'a Situation, for a Hospital, cannot be given within either of the Works at the Berry Head, as the Defences are already Choked by Barracks, & Buildings, of every description'. He suggested an extra-mural site that was 'in all respects, Eligible, as it is in a Valley from 50 to 100 feet under all the Lines of Fire – And another advantage is, that any Aspect may be given to the Front of the Building.' In other words, the sheltered position gave opportunities for a freer, non-defensive design. In October, Mercer, on behalf of the Board of Ordnance, ordered that Roger Hyne of Brixham be given permission to 'Quarry Stone, Dig Sand, and erect a small Lime Kiln, near the Spot, pointed out by me, on which to erect a Barrack Hospital'. As it turned out, construction of the hospital was a precautionary exercise: no action was seen here, though there was doubtless the occasional 'friendly fire' mishap and the sea air would have been valued as a restorative for more mundane convalescents. Above all this was a functional building: unostentatious, sturdily built from Devonian limestone rubble.

But its spectacular position made it an obvious candidate for conversion to a private residence once Napoleon had been defeated and the invasion threat had receded. Here we have, then, an early example of residential reuse of a disused public building, anticipating the many similar conversions of the late twentieth century.

Disposal by the Board of Ordnance was a fraught and protracted business – assets such military hospitals with potential for use as barracks were not lightly given up – but in 1833 Berry Head House became the home of the Scottish hymn-writer and divine Henry Francis Lyte, who composed *Abide With Me* in the grounds and created here one of the finest libraries in the south-west. Now, still in a sylvan setting, the building does service as an hotel on the peaceful, palm-fringed English Riviera.

Watercolour, unknown artist, 9 April 1861; 9 × 7 ins

Kings Weston, Somerset

This sketch, sepia-toned and highlighted with white tints in impasto, is by William Daniell RA (1769–1837) and may be assumed to have been dashed off during his mammoth decade-long progress around the country from 1813–23 to record coastal scenes. Starting in the south-west, he passed through Somerset and Gloucestershire in 1814, en route to Glamorgan. This might have been intended as a preparatory sketch, but if so it was not one he chose to work up into one of his typically polished aquatints. These he published in 1825 under the title *Voyage Round Great Britain*, the original copper plates from which were rediscovered in 1962, having been lost for a century, and are now in the Tate collection.

Our sketch is inscribed *verso 'Dist View of ye House at Kings Weston, Wm. Daniell R.A.'* and shows the view south-west over the Avon to Portishead Down and the mouth of the Severn beyond. Daniell has chosen the same angle and distance as Johannes Kip, whose bird's-eye view of a century before (1712) shows the old Tudor house, with its formal planting, just before demolition. Daniell's vantage point, though slightly elevated, is too low for much of the replacement house by Vanbrugh, finished in 1725, to be visible above the trees. What we see are Vanbrugh's powerfully massed chimneystacks, which give monumentality, especially in long views such as this, to what is a comparatively small house.

Kings Weston is, though, largely incidental in the composition, or at any rate is not its sole focus. Daniell was first and foremost a landscape painter. His main interest here is in recording topography on the one hand; then atmospheric effects – the scudding rainstorm moving inland and the brightness to the west, casting light on the house; then activity, in the shape of ships navigating the Avon, deftly caught with a few flicks of the brush; and finally local life, personified here in the shepherd in his Regency topper watching his flock. It is a sylvan, bucolic scene, but not a somnolent one. Today it is not really any of those things. Although the immediate setting of Kings Weston, and the house itself, are intact, they are caught up in the western extremity of the Bristol conurbation, with the industrial sprawl of Avonmouth covering much of the plain below.

It is fitting that the watercolour should now have a home at Fitzroy Square; it has probably been hereabouts before, as Daniell lived in nearby Howland Street from 1794 with his uncle Thomas, also a Royal Academician, and in 1825 published his *magnum opus*, *Voyage Round Great Britain*, from Russell Court, a now-lost yard just off the Square.

Watercolour by William Daniell RA (1769–1837); 7 × 5 ins

Kingsgate, Kent

One of the distinctive qualities of the Pardoe Collection is the good number of works by female amateur artists, facility in drawing being an accomplishment of the cultivated gentlewoman. Often drawn during a stay at a country house, these works offer a record of buildings that is refreshingly different from the engravings typically produced for publication. If not always wholly accurate, they nonetheless provide a point of comparison with the standard contemporary record.

That is especially true here: Kingsgate was built on an absurdly spectacular site on the North Foreland – perilously close to the cliff edge and surrounded by fantastical follies – with the result that most other depictions are distant oblique views that concentrate on highlighting the drama of the context. Ours, intriguingly, does the reverse, being a sober, almost prosaic full-frontal safely executed within the confines of the grounds.

Our artist is Emma Bennett, daughter of Richard Bennett of Beckenham in Kent and niece of Frances, Duchess of Northumberland. In 1787 she married Sir John Swinburne, 6th Bart; this sketch was completed three years before and is signed and dated, verso, 'Em Sept 28th 1784'.

That the drawing has been cut down (making the house as shown asymmetrical) suggests something of the scale of its subject, a nineteen bay seat commissioned in 1762 by the first Lord Holland, father of Charles James Fox, from the amateur architect Thomas Wynn, later first Lord Newborough (1736–1807). It is thus a young man's work, and as a young man at the time might Wynn copied from the Antique, recreating for the Kent coast a version of Tully's Formian Villa at Baiae. Either side of the Doric portico are flint bays (rendered a sort of cornflower blue by Miss Bennett, as if stuccoed); these are articulated by richly-modelled entrances, with white marble *basso-relievos*. As if the house were not advertisement enough, Holland drew further attention with his follies scattered about the landscape. Naturally, his enemies (of whom there were plenty – as secretary for war and then paymaster of the forces in Bute's ministry, Holland was known as 'the defaulter of unaccounted millions') saw an opportunity for derision. Horace Walpole thought that it might be mistaken 'for a prospect in some half-civilised island discovered by Captain Cook'. And Thomas Gray (*On Ld H-'s Seat near M-, K-,*1768) adopted the heroic couplet form of verse essay to stick the knife in further: '*Old and abandoned by each venal friend / Here H[olland] took the pious resolution / To smuggle some few years and strive to mend / A broken character and constitution. / On this congenial spot he fixed his choice; Earl Godwin trembled for his neighbouring sand; / …Now mouldering fanes and battlements arise, / Arches and turrets nodding to their fall, / Unpeopled palaces delude his eyes, / And mimic desolation covers all…*'

The house fell prey to speculators shortly after Holland's death; by 1807 the portico had gone to the Royal Sea Bathing Hospital in Margate and Holland House, as it had become known, was later largely demolished. What survives are the three right-hand bays, still recognisable as part of an 1850s pile called, fittingly, Holland's End.

Watercolour by Emma Bennett, September 28th 1784; 17 × 11 ins

Cheam School, Surrey

Our unsigned pen and wash sketch shows Cheam School in Surrey, probably in the mid-1780s based on internal evidence: the etiolated Modigliani figures sport tailcoats and tricorns of that period and the inscription (*the Revd. Mr. Wilson's Semenery* [sic] *at Cheam. The Right Hble Wm Pitt & other great statesmen educated in this Semenary*) requires a date after Pitt might be said to have achieved greatness, say in 1783. It is possible that the rather clumsy inscription was added later, after the career of the one other Georgian pupil who has claim to be a great statesman – Viscount Sidmouth, Prime Minister 1801–1804 – had reached its zenith.

As a boy Pitt the Younger was educated at home owing to persistent ill-health. Rosebery's *Pitt* (1899) says that 'from six to fourteen [when he went up to Cambridge] his health was so indifferent that for more than half that period he was unable to apply himself to study'. No biography records him attending a school, but Edward Wilson was certainly one of his tutors. Wilson is recorded by Pretyman as saying that Pitt seemed 'never…to learn, but merely to recollect'. By all accounts, though, Wilson and his fellow tutors achieved remarkable success, albeit with extraordinarily precocious raw material. Rosebery records that Pitt's 'proficiency in the learned languages was probably greater than ever was acquired by any other person in such early youth; it was no uncommon thing for him to read into English six or seven pages of Thucydides, which he had not previously seen, without more than two or three mistakes, and sometimes without even one.'

Whether or not the scene of Pitt's early education, the red brick building we see here housed a highly reputable school from its construction in 1719. It was purpose-built as a school to accommodate the transfer of what was then Manor House School from Whitehill, a weatherboarded Tudor house in Cheam that survives to this day. The school had been set up in the 1640s by the Revd. George Aldrich and prospered after the Restoration, not only because Aldrich had been a Royalist during the Commonwealth but also because the downland air provided respite from London's foetid air during the plague. In its handsome early Georgian home it continued to thrive: from 1752 to 1777 its headmaster was William Gilpin, lampooned as Dr. Syntax by William Combe and caricatured by Rowlandson but a serious theorist of the picturesque.

Though modified and extended by the Victorians – it was converted to a pioneering prep school by A. S. Tabor, Headmaster in the 1850s – its façade remained largely as depicted here until the early twentieth century. The inter-war expansion and suburbanisation of Cheam, which brought with it road-widening, a bypass and encroaching development, prompted the school to move to Berkshire in 1934. The Duke of Edinburgh was one of the last pupils to occupy the building before its demolition in 1935. Only the Victorian Chapel, now a Roman Catholic Church, survives, amid a housing development named after Mr Tabor.

The Rev.ᵈ Mʳ. Wilson's Semenary at Cheam.
& other great Statesmen educated in this Semenary.

The Right Hble Wᵐ Pitt

Sketch'd

Pen and wash, unknown artist, c.1785; 7 × 5 ins

Quidenham Hall, Norfolk

Quidenham, between Thetford and Norwich, is shown here in its Victorian heyday - although its footprint is considerably bigger today, a Carmelite monastery having been grafted on, among the trees to the left, in the 1950s. The building volume is exaggerated in this depiction, the artist having skewed the perspective almost as if using axonometric projection; the right-hand elevation is in fact on a single plane, not splayed as shown here. This primitive treatment, probably more a result of lack of skill than design, has the accidental virtue of allowing two elevations at right angles to each other to be shown as if in linear progression. The result is both naïve and canny: a misrepresentation that nonetheless allows the exterior detail to be read more clearly.

As the building survives in a landscaped setting (planting rather than development has obscured this particular viewpoint), direct comparisons are straightforward. An additional storey has at some point been squeezed in either side of the portico, although both apsidal bays remain two-storey; and a simple lawn now stands in place of the mid-Victorian parterre – probably a new intervention at the time of this watercolour, hence its prominence in the view, with the pelargoniums (favourites of Queen Victoria) given more or less equal billing with the house. It is hard to escape the conclusion the artist hoped to achieve at least as much a horticultural as an architectural record. The most significant interloper, the monastic complex, has institutionalised the house to some degree and almost doubled its size but was added in a sympathetic red-brick idiom, its pared-down design, cloister plan and deferential massing allowing it to sit harmoniously with the main house despite its volume.

The arrival of the Carmelites after the Second War was the latest stage in the evolution of a multi-phase house built by the Protestant Thomas Holland in 1606 on the site of a manor house acquired from the recusant Bedingfields, themselves too beleaguered by religious persecution to keep it on. In 1740 the Hollands sold to the Portuguese wine merchant John Bristow, who added the classical east and west fronts, the latter (facing the viewer in this watercolour) with a powerful Ionic portico. The linking south front, late eighteenth century, is articulated with a central recession accommodating a Tuscan porch.

The interior includes good early seventeenth century strapwork and a fine library of 1820 by C. Heathcote Tatham commissioned by the Keppels, Earls of Albemarle, who bought Quidenham when their rise in fortunes (the third earl enriched himself by conquering Havana in 1762 during the Seven Years' War) coincided with the Bristows' impoverishment after the Lisbon earthquake of 1755. The Keppels kept the house until 1948, when punitive post-war conditions forced another sale. In such circumstances it might easily have joined the long list of houses lost in the middle of the twentieth century, but divine intervention brought the Carmelites of Rushmere, who gave it renewed life as a nunnery and hospice.

Watercolour, initialled 'EJS', August 11th 1863; 11 × 5 ins

Rochford Hall, Essex

The inscribing of 'Rochford Hall' on the foreground tombstone is perhaps just an artist's conceit, using the convenient form of the stone as a cartouche, but it might also be a kind of epitaph for a house that by the mid-nineteenth century had reached near-terminal decline. As it turned out, rumours of its death were exaggerated, but our Victorian watercolourist might have supposed himself to be recording a threatened house for posterity.

There is, in fact, much about Rochford that is lapidary. Apocryphally, it is the scene of Henry VIII's clandestine meetings with Anne Boleyn and thus has claim to be the birthplace of the Reformation; Henry is supposed to have come and gone by secret tunnel, no evident trace of which remains. But neither does much remain of the moated Tudor courtyard house, of which our picture shows only the north-eastern corner, the rump that survived a huge fire in 1760 and piecemeal losses thereafter.

The form of the Tudor building is partly conjectural, but it is a reasonable guess that, at its greatest extent, the elevation shown here had another four bays to the left, with a projecting central gatehouse and turreted towers at either end. The fire put paid to the symmetry and also to the aggrandising ambition of successive owners. The house had passed from the 1530s through the Boleyns to the kindred Careys and the Riches, who bankrolled expansion and remodelling in the early seventeenth century, and then to the Childs, Earls Tynley

of Wanstead, on whose watch the catastrophic fire happened. It might then, like Wanstead, have been consigned to history, but the 2nd Earl merely reduced its size and converted parts to barns. In the 1860s it was bought by the farmer James Tabor when on the cusp of dereliction.

Our amateur artist, then, has recorded a vulnerable but fascinating fragment. Admittedly, he has not done so with huge spatial accuracy: for dramatic effect, the perspective has been foreshortened so that the churchyard of St Andrew's Rochford appears closer to the house than it is. But essentially the scene today remains as depicted here. The house now serves as a golf clubhouse, with the north-western wing partly reinstated as private houses, and the estate, pockmarked with bunkers, joins up with Southend airport to form a buffer of sorts between Rochford and Southend.

Watercolour, unknown artist; 7.7 × 5 ins

Oxton House, Devon

Our watercolour of Oxton has been crudely cut on both sides to fit an album but the date is clear – 1796 – and the signature, though cropped to leave no more than the initials, is that of the Revd. John Swete, an accomplished watercolourist who between 1789 and 1801 toured the south-western counties, filling twenty volumes of diaries with over six hundred watercolours of houses, antiquities and other features of picturesque interest. His inspiration was that other itinerant artist-cum-cleric, the Revd. William Gilpin, whose *Observations* series, part of his visual manifesto for the picturesque movement, was published from the 1780s. In that sense Swete's output could be seen as derivative, both in style and composition – the careful framing of the distant house by trees, accentuating the landscape, is a typical device – but perhaps it is better viewed as homage paid by a disciple.

Certainly Swete was accomplished enough to hold his own in august company. This watercolour has a sketchy quality characteristic of one dashed off *en plein air*, but it shows verve and technical proficiency. And although it carries a sense of having been casually drawn, as if the artist on his peregrination had chanced upon this vista and taken up his brush in wonderment, this was a view lodged firmly in Swete's mind. Indeed, it was largely his creation. Oxton, marching with Mamhead on the eastern edge of Haldon Moor, had passed to his father from a cousin in 1767; John inherited in 1781, giving him the perfect opportunity to indulge his modish passion for landscape design. By 1793 his fellow vicar Richard Polwhele, with whom he founded a literary and historical circle in Exeter, was able to remark approvingly that the grounds at Oxton were 'laid out in a style that perfectly accords with the modern fashion in gardening … since it is founded on the principles of NATURE and TRUTH'. In fact, of course, it was highly contrived, a model of artifice that might be said to have improved on nature, but the moral dimension was not one to have escaped a man of the cloth.

Swete did not, in fact, stop at the landscape. He also demolished the sixteenth century manor house and replaced it with the plain stuccoed country house shown here, the only architectural flourish the canted bays designed to maximise the newly-opened views of the landscape. The house is very much an extra in this drama: the sylvan idyll takes centre-stage. The external appearance was too sober for succeeding generations, and one of the points of interest of this watercolour is that it shows the house as originally built. By the 1830s, shortly after Swete's death, titivation was already in train: a loggia was added between the canted bays and the south façade (on the left here) was embellished with a Doric portico in the Greek Revival style. This latter was removed in the mid twentieth century, when Oxton was converted to apartments after a time as a girls' boarding school, but in their essentials the house and landscape survive today much as recorded here, a relict of the late Georgian enthusiasm for the picturesque.

Watercolour, by the Revd. John Swete, 1796; 7 × 5 ins

Beaudesert Stables, Staffordshire

Beaudesert is a kind of exemplar of the tribulations suffered by English country houses in the twentieth century. Burnt down in 1909, it was lavishly and very convincingly resurrected on the eve of the Great War, before a combination of punitive taxation, economic depression and reckless spending by the 'Dancing' Marquess of Anglesey led to the dissolution of the estate. Failing to find a buyer, it was largely demolished in 1935, with some interiors, including the Waterloo Staircase, reassembled in South Australia and the better bricks used to reface the pollution-ravaged walls of St James's Palace. Only shattered fragments now survive.

The Edwardians, being virtuoso Mannerists, had painstakingly recreated the Tudor interiors that the Georgians, in the 1770s, had in part replaced with light and delicate rooms by Wyatt – froth and frippery, as the sober-minded faux-mediaevalists of a century and more ago saw it. What survived this succession of making and unmaking was the 1770s stable and coach block illustrated here. It is hardly an accomplished drawing and the attribution *verso* (in the form of a dealer's stamp) to 'Moses Griffith b1747 d1819 from the Thomas Pennant and Earl of Denbigh collections' must be doubted. Griffith (in fact born in 1749) was a skilled draughtsman and even for a sketch this piece seems too clumsy and ill-proportioned to be plausibly his. The name of the house – roughly meaning 'beautiful wilderness' – is also misspelt.

Nonetheless, the picture gives us an intriguing glimpse of an estate building that is largely overshadowed in the documentary record by the Tudor-cum-Edwardian house. Contemporary with the Wyatt interior remodelling, it provides a link in the design progression of the stable as a Georgian building type, when it moved fairly swiftly from being a wing of the house (*à la* Palladio) to a detached courtyard block in the Houghton manner and then a fully-realised and independent architectural element adjacent to the house. Finally, as here, it became a freestanding, almost picturesque conceit out of sight and earshot.

The Beaudesert stables are too early for Repton, who made his first serious forays into landscaping about ten years later – and indeed produced a Red Book for Beaudesert that survives at Princeton – but it anticipates some of his thinking. The building groups together all the messy activity of coach house and stables, which are thoroughly integrated when traditionally they had been left separate, and moves them a safe and discreet distance from the house, which can then be left in unsullied repose as an aesthetic object in the landscape. Repton did much the same at Harlestone in Northamptonshire in 1810.

The complex looks almost abandoned here – an unattended chaise is the only sign of life – but the drawing conveys a sense of the building as a coherent, considered architectural composition: the cool stone, the unusual crescent configuration (such a departure from the usual severe barrack-block form) and the setting within a contrived landscape all speak of a highly functional building given assured aesthetic treatment.

Beaudesert Stables

Pen and wash, unknown artist; 9 × 6 ins

THE
GEORGIAN
GROUP

The Georgian Group is the national charity
dedicated to preserving Georgian buildings
and gardens – one of Britain's greatest assets.

Every year it is consulted on several thousand
planning applications involving demolition or
alterations. Its intervention has helped save
many Georgian buildings and protect others
from unsympathetic alterations.

New members are welcome. You can join
online at www.georgiangroup.org.uk